Best Kids' KNOCK-KNOCK Jokes EVER!

VOLUME 1

JOKES TO KNOCK
YOUR SOCKS OFF!

Highlights Press
Honesdale, Pennsylvania

Cover Design by Colleen Pidell
Contributing Illustrators: David Coulson, Kelly Kennedy, Pat N. Lewis, Neil Numberman, Rich Powell, Kevin Rechin, Rick Stromoski, Pete Whitehead

Published by Highlights Press
815 Church Street
Honesdale, Pennsylvania 18431
ISBN: 978-1-68437-245-4
Manufactured in Grand Rapids, MI, USA
Mfg. 03/2025

First edition
Visit our website at Highlights.com.
10 9 8

CONTENTS

LAUGHS FOR LUNCH

Knock, knock.

Who's there?

Pizza.

Pizza who?

Pizza really nice guy.

Knock, knock.

Who's there?

Pudding.

Pudding who?

Pudding on your shoes before your pants is a bad idea.

Knock, knock.

Who's there?

Cheese.

Cheese who?

Cheese a very smart girl.

Knock, knock.

Who's there?

Pasta.

Pasta who?

Pasta salt and pepper, please.

Knock, knock.

Who's there?

Achoo.

Achoo who?

Achoo my gum every day.

Knock, knock.

Who's there?

Broccoli.

Broccoli who?

Broccoli doesn't have a last name, silly.

Knock, knock.

Who's there?

Alec.

Alec who?

Alec tea, but I don't like coffee.

Knock, knock.

Who's there?

Ketchup.

Ketchup who?

Ketchup with me and I'll tell you.

Knock, knock.

Who's there?

Jupiter.

Jupiter who?

Jupiter fly in my soup?

Knock, knock.

Who's there?

Handsome.

Handsome who?

Handsome of those cookies over, please. I'm hungry.

Knock, knock.

Who's there?

Falafel.

Falafel who?

I falafel my bike and hurt my knee.

Knock, knock.

Who's there?

Window.

Window who?

Window we eat?

Knock, knock.

Who's there?

Soda.

Soda who?

Soda answer is still no?

Knock, knock.

Who's there?

Mushroom.

Mushroom who?

There's mushroom for improvement on that last joke.

Knock, knock.

Who's there?

Hammond.

Hammond who?

Hammond eggs for breakfast.

Knock, knock.

Who's there?

Banana.

Banana who?

Knock, knock.

Who's there?

Banana.

Banana who?

Knock, knock.

Who's there?

Orange.

Orange who?

Orange you glad I didn't say banana?

Knock, knock.

Who's there?

Pecan.

Pecan who?

Pecan somebody your own size!

Knock, knock.

Who's there?

Howdy.

Howdy who?

Howdy-licious are those cookies?

Knock, knock.

Who's there?

Sophie.

Sophie who?

I'm hungry, Sophie me.

Knock, knock.

Who's there?

Beets.

Beets who?

Beets me.

Knock, knock.

Who's there?

Toast.

Toast who?

Toast were the days.

Knock, knock.

Who's there?

Distressing.

Distressing who?

Distressing has too much vinegar.

Knock, knock.

Who's there?

Cash.

Cash who?

**No, thanks.
I prefer peanuts.**

Knock, knock.

Who's there?

Bean.

Bean who?

Bean fishing lately?

Knock, knock.

Who's there?

Omelet.

Omelet who?

Omelet smarter than you think.

Knock, knock.

Who's there?

Fajita.

Fajita who?

Fajita another thing, I'll be stuffed.

Knock, knock.

Who's there?

Mint.

Mint who?

I mint to tell you sooner that I was coming over.

Knock, knock.

Who's there?

Stew.

Stew who?

Stew early to go to bed.

Knock, knock.

Who's there?

Sauce.

Sauce who?

He sauce together yesterday.

Knock, knock.

Who's there?

Japan.

Japan who?

Ouch, Japan is too hot.

Knock, knock.

Who's there?

Avocado.

Avocado who?

Avocado an awful cold. Achoo!

Knock, knock.

Who's there?

Nacho cheese.

Nacho cheese who?

That is nacho cheese, so give it back!

Knock, knock.

Who's there?

Ham.

Ham who?

Ham I getting warmer?

Knock, knock.

Who's there?

Orange.

Orange who?

Orange you going to let me in?

ANIMAL ANTICS

Knock, knock.

Who's there?

Poodle.

Poodle who?

Poodle little mustard on my hot dog.

Knock, knock.

Who's there?

Rhino.

Rhino who?

Rhino lots of good knock-knock jokes.

Knock, knock.

Who's there?

Whale.

Whale who?

Whale, whale, whale. I see your door is locked again.

Knock, knock.

Who's there?

Earwig.

Earwig who?

Earwig go again.

Knock, knock.

Who's there?

Bunny.

Bunny who?

Bunny thing is, I've forgotten!

Knock, knock.

Who's there?

Ostrich.

Ostrich who?

Ostrich my arms up to the sky.

Knock, knock.

Who's there?

Cock-a-doodle.

Cock-a-doodle who?

Not cock-a-doodle who, you silly chicken, *cock-a-doodle-doo*!

Knock, knock.

Who's there?

Turtle.

Turtle who?

Got to go. Turtle-oo!

Knock, knock.

Who's there?

Gorilla.

Gorilla who?

Gorilla cheese sandwich for me, if you please.

Knock, knock.

Who's there?

Me.

Me who?

You sure have a funny-sounding cat.

Knock, knock.

Who's there?

Goose.

Goose who?

No, you goose who!

Knock, knock.

Who's there?

Newt.

Newt who?

What's newt with you?

Knock, knock.

Who's there?

Otter.

Otter who?

You otter open the door and let me in.

Knock, knock.

Who's there?

Deduct.

Deduct who?

Deduct went, "Quack, quack."

Knock, knock.

Who's there?

Amos.

Amos who?

A mosquito.

Knock, knock.

Who's there?

Grrr.

Grrr who?

Are you a bear or an owl?

Knock, knock.

Who's there?

Sheep.

Sheep who?

Sheep-ers! It's just me.

Knock, knock.

Who's there?

Spider.

Spider who?

**In spider everything,
I still like you.**

Knock, knock.

Who's there?

Worm.

Worm who?

It's worm in here, isn't it?

Knock, knock.

Who's there?

Champ.

Champ who?

**Champ-oo the dog.
He needs a bath!**

Knock, knock.

Who's there?

Aurora.

Aurora who?

Aurora's just come from that big polar bear.

Knock, knock.

Who's there?

Gnu.

Gnu who?

Gnu you'd ask me that.

Knock, knock.

Who's there?

Koala.

Koala who?

These are some koala-ty knock-knock jokes!

Knock, knock.

Who's there?

Cow.

Cow who?

Cow much longer are you going to put up with all this knocking?

Knock, knock.

Who's there?

Toad.

Toad who?

Toad you I knew some good knock-knock jokes.

DO-RE-ME-HEE-HEE

Knock, knock.

Who's there?

Sing.

Sing who?

Whoooooo!

Knock, knock.

Who's there?

Shelby.

Shelby who?

"Shelby comin' round the mountain when she comes!"

Knock, knock.

Who's there?

Tuba.

Tuba who?

Tuba toothpaste.

Knock, knock.

Who's there?

Mozart.

Mozart who?

Mozart is found in museums.

Knock, knock.

Who's there?

Fiddle.

Fiddle who?

Fiddle make you happy, I'll tell you.

Knock, knock.

Who's there?

Duet.

Duet who?

Duet yourself and quit bothering me!

Knock, knock.

Who's there?

Abandon.

Abandon who?

Abandon the street is marching this way.

Knock, knock.

Who's there?

Cello.

Cello who?

Cello there!

Knock, knock.

Who's there?

Sonata.

Sonata who?

Don't worry, sonata big deal.

Knock, knock.

Who's there?

Benjamin.

Benjamin who?

Benjamin with the band all night.

Knock, knock.

Who's there?

Accordion.

Accordion who?

Accordion the weather report, it's going to rain tomorrow.

Knock, knock.

Who's there?

Tuna.

Tuna who?

Tuna piano and it'll sound better.

Knock, knock.

Who's there?

Rupert.

Rupert who?

"Rupert your left foot in, Rupert your left foot out."

Knock, knock.

Who's there?

Bach.

Bach who?

Bach to work!

SCHOOL-ARIOUS!

Knock, knock.

Who's there?

Rice.

Rice who?

Rice and shine! It's the first day of school.

Knock, knock.

Who's there?

Needle.

Needle who?

Needle little help with your homework?

Knock, knock.

Who's there?

Decay.

Decay who?

Decay is after de J in the alphabet.

Knock, knock.

Who's there?

Ketchup.

Ketchup who?

Ketchup or else you'll miss the school bus!

Knock, knock.

Who's there?

Hallways.

Hallways who?

Why are you hallways late?

Knock, knock.

Who's there?

Pencil.

Pencil who?

Pencil fall down if you don't wear a belt.

Knock, knock.

Who's there?

Spell.

Spell who?

W-H-O.

Knock, knock.

Who's there?

Atlas.

Atlas who?

Atlas, it's the weekend!

Knock, knock.

Who's there?

Wafer.

Wafer who?

Wafer the bus at the corner.

Knock, knock.

Who's there?

Justin.

Justin who?

Justin time for recess.

Knock, knock.

Who's there?

Wanda.

Wanda who?

I Wanda where I put my homework.

Knock, knock.

Who's there?

To.

To who?

No! It's "to whom."

Knock, knock.

Who's there?

Prod.

Prod who?

Prod of you for getting an A.

Knock, knock.

Who's there?

Raisin.

Raisin who?

We're raisin our hands before we speak.

Knock, knock.

Who's there?

Geometry.

Geometry who?

Geometry in the school play!

Knock, knock.

Who's there?

Tamara.

Tamara who?

Tamara is another school day.

LETTUCE IN! (WHO'S AT THE DOOR?)

Knock, knock.

Who's there?

Dishes.

Dishes who?

Dishes me. Can I come in?

Knock, knock.

Who's there?

Lettuce.

Lettuce who?

Lettuce in! It's cold out here.

Knock, knock.

Who's there?

Statue.

Statue who?

It's me. Statue?

Knock, knock.

Who's there?

Apple.

Apple who?

Apple on the door, but it doesn't open.

Knock, knock.

Who's there?

Justice.

Justice who?

**Justice I thought—
no one home.**

Knock, knock.

Who's there?

Sherlock.

Sherlock who?

Sherlock the door. See if I care.

Knock, knock.

Who's there?

Dozen.

Dozen who?

**Dozen anyone want to
let me in?**

Knock, knock.

Who's there?

Wendy.

Wendy who?

Wendy bell works again, I won't have to knock anymore.

Knock, knock.

Who's there?

Wooden shoe.

Wooden shoe who?

Wooden shoe like to know?

Knock, knock.

Who's there?

Major.

Major who?

Major open the door, didn't I?

Knock, knock.

Who's there?

Water.

Water who?

Water you waiting for? Let me in.

Knock, knock.

Who's there?

Ben.

Ben who?

Ben knocking for twenty minutes!

Knock, knock.

Who's there?

A little boy.

A little boy who?

A little boy who can't reach the doorbell.

Knock, knock.

Who's there?

Adore.

Adore who?

Adore is between us. Open up!

Knock, knock.

Who's there?

Arnold.

Arnold who?

Arnold friend you haven't seen in years.

Knock, knock.

Who's there?

Ear.

Ear who?

Ear you are! I've been looking everywhere.

Knock, knock.

Who's there?

Cozy.

Cozy who?

Cozy who's knocking.

Knock, knock.

Who's there?

Bean.

Bean who?

Bean here for ages. What's kept you?

Knock, knock.

Who's there?

Dill.

Dill who?

Good-bye dill we meet again.

WHAT'S IN A NAME?

Knock, knock.

Who's there?

Emma.

Emma who?

Emma bit cold out here—please let me in.

Knock, knock.

Who's there?

Aaron.

Aaron who?

Aaron the barber's floor.

Knock, knock.

Who's there?

Alex.

Alex who?

Alex the questions around here!

Knock, knock.

Who's there?

Allison.

Allison who?

Allison to you if you'll listen to me.

Knock, knock.

Who's there?

Althea.

Althea who?

Althea later, dude.

Knock, knock.

Who's there?

Annette.

Annette who?

Annette to use the bathroom, so please open the door!

Knock, knock.

Who's there?

Beth.

Beth who?

I didn't sneeze!

Knock, knock.

Who's there?

Carmen.

Carmen who?

Carmen get it.

Knock, knock.

Who's there?

Claire.

Claire who?

**Claire the way,
I'm coming through!**

Knock, knock.

Who's there?

Colin.

Colin who?

Just Colin to tell you another great knock-knock joke!

Knock, knock.

Who's there?

Colleen.

Colleen who?

Colleen up your room. It's a mess!

Knock, knock.

Who's there?

Diego.

Diego who?

Diego before de B.

Knock, knock.

Who's there?

Dwight.

Dwight who?

There's Dwight way and there's de wrong way.

Knock, knock.

Who's there?

Eileen.

Eileen who?

Eileen over to tie my shoes.

Knock, knock.

Who's there?

Felix.

Felix who?

Felix my ice cream again, he'll be in trouble.

Knock, knock.

Who's there?

Fitzwilliam.

Fitzwilliam who?

Fitzwilliam better than it fits me.

Knock, knock.

Who's there?

Freddie.

Freddie who?

Freddie or not, here I come.

Knock, knock.

Who's there?

Hugo.

Hugo who?

Hugo first and I'll go second.

Knock, knock.

Who's there?

Jess.

Jess who?

Jess me and my shadow.

Knock, knock.

Who's there?

Lisa.

Lisa who?

Lisa you can do is let me in.

Knock, knock.

Who's there?

Luke.

Luke who?

Luke before you leap.

Knock, knock.

Who's there?

Maya.

Maya

Maya best friend?

Knock, knock.

Who's there?

Matthew.

Matthew who?

Matthew is pinthing my foot.

Knock, knock.

Who's there?

Max.

Max who?

Max no difference to me!

Knock, knock.

Who's there?

Megan.

Megan who?

You're Megan me crazy with all these knock-knock jokes.

Knock, knock.

Who's there?

Nadia.

Nadia who?

Nadia head if you understand what I'm saying.

Knock, knock.

Who's there?

Oscar.

Oscar who?

Oscar silly question, get a silly answer.

Knock, knock.

Who's there?

Sarah.

Sarah who?

Sarah reason you're not laughing?

Knock, knock.

Who's there?

Sasha.

Sasha who?

You make Sasha fuss!

Knock, knock.

Who's there?

Scott.

Scott who?

There's Scott to be a better knock-knock joke than this one!

Knock, knock.

Who's there?

Stephanie.

Stephanie who?

It's Stephanie going to be sunny today.

Knock, knock.

Who's there?

Taylor.

Taylor who?

Taylor little sister to pick up her toys.

Knock, knock.

Who's there?

Toby.

Toby who?

Toby, or not Toby, that is the question.

Knock, knock.

Who's there?

Vaughn.

Vaughn who?

Vaughn plus Vaughn equals two.

Knock, knock.

Who's there?

Xavier.

Xavier who?

Xavier money for a rainy day.

SPORTS, OF COURSE!

Knock, knock.

Who's there?

Meow.

Meow who?

"Take meow to the ballgame."

Knock, knock.

Who's there?

Tennis.

Tennis who?

Tennis five plus five.

Knock, knock.

Who's there?

Pasta.

Pasta who?

Pasta ball—I'm open!

Knock, knock.

Who's there?

Rush hour.

Rush hour who?

Rush hour quarterback and we'll block you.

Knock, knock.

Who's there?

Randy.

Randy who?

Randy mile in eight minutes.

Knock, knock.

Who's there?

Anya.

Anya who?

Anya mark, get set, go!

Knock, knock.

Who's there?

Uriah.

Uriah who?

Keep Uriah on the ball.

Knock, knock.

Who's there?

Scold.

Scold who?

Scold enough to go ice skating.

Knock, knock.

Who's there?

Adolph.

Adolph who?

Adolph ball hit me in the mowf!

Knock, knock.

Who's there?

Dissenter.

Dissenter who?

Dissenter fielder catches a lot of fly balls.

Knock, knock.

Who's there?

Andy.

Andy who?

Andy shoots, Andy scores!

Knock, knock.

Who's there?

Alana.

Alana who?

Alana my head after I tripped over your skateboard!

Knock, knock.

Who's there?

Bjorn.

Bjorn who?

Bjorn to run.

Knock, knock.

Who's there?

Omega.

Omega who?

Omega best player win.

Knock, knock.

Who's there?

Phillip.

Philip who?

Phillip your pool. I want to go swimming!

Knock, knock.

Who's there?

Grape.

Grape who?

Grape game you played today!

Knock, knock.

Who's there?

Tummy.

Tummy who?

Tummy you'll always be number one.

TICKLISH FAIRY TALES

Knock, knock.

Who's there?

Never Never Land.

Never Never Land who?

Never Never Land money to a stranger.

Knock, knock.

Who's there?

Mara.

Mara who?

"Mara, Mara on the wall . . ."

Knock, knock.

Who's there?

Myth.

Myth who?

Myth you, too.

Knock, knock.

Who's there?

Fairy.

Fairy who?

Fairy pleased to meet you!

Knock, knock.

Who's there?

Lee King.

Lee King who?

Lee King bucket.

Knock, knock.

Who's there?

Dragon.

Dragon who?

Dragon arm chair over here and let's talk.

Knock, knock.

Who's there?

Ogre.

Ogre who?

I'm ogre here! Come find me.

Knock, knock.

Who's there?

Castle.

Castle who?

You castle lot of questions, don't you?

Knock, knock.

Who's there?

Garden.

Garden who?

A dragon is garden the treasure.

Knock, knock.

Who's there?

Queen.

Queen who?

Queen as a whistle.

Knock, knock.

Who's there?

Tinkerbell.

Tinkerbell who?

Tinkerbell is out of order.

Knock, knock.

Who's there?

Unite.

Unite who?

When unite Lancelot, he joins the Round Table.

Knock, knock.

Who's there?

Knights.

Knights who?

Knights to meet you!

Knock, knock.

Who's there?

Armor.

Armor who?

Armor snacks coming? I'm starving!

Knock, knock.

Who's there?

Fantasy.

Fantasy who?

Fantasy-ing you here!

Knock, knock.

Who's there?

Hugh.

Hugh who?

Hugh's afraid of the big, bad wolf?

Knock, knock.

Who's there?

Vaughn.

Vaughn who?

Vaughn day my prince will come.

Knock, knock.

Who's there?

Goblin.

Goblin who?

Goblin your food will give you a tummyache.

Knock, knock.

Who's there?

Dragon.

Dragon who?

These jokes are dragon on and on.

Knock, knock.

Who's there?

Interrupting pirate.

Interrup—

ARRRRR!

Knock, knock.

Who's there?

Kissimmee.

Kissimmee who?

Kissimmee a frog and he'll turn into a prince!

Knock, knock.

Who's there?

Olive.

Olive who?

And they olive happily ever after.

WHEELY FUNNY

Knock, knock.

Who's there?

Cargo.

Cargo who?

Cargo *beep, beep*!

Knock, knock.

Who's there?

Wheel.

Wheel who?

Wheel be going now. Good-bye!

Knock, knock.

Who's there?

Rowan.

Rowan who?

Rowan a boat is hard work.

Knock, knock.

Who's there?

Diesel.

Diesel who?

Diesel be the best cookies ever.

Knock, knock.

Who's there?

Isabelle.

Isabelle who?

Isabelle on your bike?

Knock, knock.

Who's there?

Phillip.

Phillip who?

Phillip my gas tank, please. I've got a long way to go.

Knock, knock.

Who's there?

Carlotta.

Carlotta who?

Carlotta trouble when it breaks down.

Knock, knock.

Who's there?

Leslie.

Leslie who?

Leslie town and take the train.

Knock, knock.

Who's there?

Canoe.

Canoe who?

Canoe come out and play?

Knock, knock.

Who's there?

Mild.

Mild who?

Mild bike was red but my new bike is blue.

Knock, knock.

Who's there?

Pumpkin.

Pumpkin who?

A pumpkin fill up your flat tire.

Knock, knock.

Who's there?

Yacht.

Yacht who?

Yacht to know me by now!

Knock, knock.

Who's there?

Micah.

Micah who?

**Micah has a flat tire—
can you help?**

Knock, knock.

Who's there?

Jethro.

Jethro who?

Jethro the boat and stop asking questions.

Knock, knock.

Who's there?

Zoom.

Zoom who?

Zoom did you expect?

Knock, knock.

Who's there?

Oil change.

Oil change who?

Oil change. Just give me another chance.

Knock, knock.

Who's there?

Tire.

Tire who?

Tire shoe before you trip!

Knock, knock.

Who's there?

Mandy.

Mandy who?

Mandy lifeboats—de ship is sinking.

Knock, knock.

Who's there?

Carl.

Carl who?

Carl get you there faster than a bike.

Knock, knock.

Who's there?

Cairo.

Cairo who?

Cairo the boat now?

Knock, knock.

Who's there?

Carson.

Carson who?

Carson the freeway drive really fast.

Knock, knock.

Who's there?

Van.

Van who?

Van can I see you again?

Knock, knock.

Who's there?

Ivan.

Ivan who?

"Ivan working on the railroad . . ."

STATELY JOKES

Knock, knock.

Who's there?

Florida.

Florida who?

The Florida bathroom is wet.

Knock, knock.

Who's there?

Tennessee.

Tennessee who?

Tennessee you later?

Knock, knock.

Who's there?

Zippy.

Zippy who?

Mrs. Zippy.

Knock, knock.

Who's there?

Iowa.

Iowa who?

Iowa you a dollar.

Knock, knock.

Who's there?

Arizona.

Arizona who?

Arizona room for one of us in this town.

Knock, knock.

Who's there?

Alaska.

Alaska who?

Alaska my mom if I can come out and play.

Knock, knock.

Who's there?

Kansas.

Kansas who?

Kansas what soda comes in.

Knock, knock.

Who's there?

Minneapolis.

Minneapolis who?

Minneapolis a day keeps many doctors away.

Knock, knock.

Who's there?

Arkansas.

Arkansas who?

Arkansas through any piece of wood in five seconds.

Knock, knock.

Who's there?

Hawaii.

Hawaii who?

Hawaii doing today?

Knock, knock.

Who's there?

Albany.

Albany who?

Albanying help with my homework!

Knock, knock.

Who's there?

Wyoming.

Wyoming who?

Wyoming so mean to me?

Knock, knock.

Who's there?

Harrisburg.

Harrisburg who?

Harrisburg-er for you.

Knock, knock.

Who's there?

Dakota.

Dakota who?

Dakota is too short in the arms for me.

Knock, knock.

Who's there?

Texas.

Texas who?

Texas are getting higher every year.

Knock, knock.

Who's there?

Utah King.

Utah King who?

Utah King to me?

Knock, knock.

Who's there?

Kentucky.

Kentucky who?

Dad Kentucky you in at night.

HOLIDAY HA-HA-HAS

Knock, knock.

Who's there?

Twig.

Twig who?

Twig or tweat?

Valentine's Day

Knock, knock.

Who's there?

Iguana.

Iguana who?

Iguana hold your hand.

Knock, knock.

Who's there?

Honeydew.

Honeydew who?

Honeydew you love me?

Knock, knock.

Who's there?

Peas.

Peas who?

Peas be my Valentine!

Knock, knock.

Who's there?

Heart.

Heart who?

It's heart to hear you—speak up.

Knock, knock.

Who's there?

Lena.

Lena who?

Lena little closer and give me a kiss.

Knock, knock.

Who's there?

Olive.

Olive who?

Olive you!

Knock, knock.

Who's there?

Tail.

Tail who?

Tail me you love me!

Knock, knock.

Who's there?

Quiche.

Quiche who?

Can I have a hug and a quiche?

Knock, knock.

Who's there?

Warrior.

Warrior who?

Warrior been all my life?

Knock, knock.

Who's there?

Ruth.

Ruth who?

The Ruth of the matter is, I like you.

Knock, knock.

Who's there?

Whale.

Whale who?

Whale you be mine?

Knock, knock.

Who's there?

Cantaloupe.

Cantaloupe who?

Cantaloupe tonight—I forgot the wedding ring.

St. Patrick's Day

Knock, knock.

Who's there?

Irish.

Irish who?

Irish you a happy St. Patrick's Day!

Knock, knock.

Who's there?

Dublin.

Dublin who?

Dublin up with laughter!

Knock, knock.

Who's there?

Sluggy.

Sluggy who?

Sluggy to find a four-leaf clover.

April Fools' Day

Knock, knock.

Who's there?

Noah.

Noah who?

Noah body. April Fools'!

Knock, knock.

Who's there?

Noah.

Noah who?

Noah body again!

Knock, knock.

Who's there?

Noah.

Noah who?

Noah joking this time. Can I come in?

Fourth of July

Knock, knock.

Who's there?

Llama.

Llama who?

"Llama Yankee Doodle Dandy."

Knock, knock.

Who's there?

Sherwood.

Sherwood who?

Sherwood like to see some fireworks!

Knock, knock.

Who's there?

José.

José who?

"José can you see . . ."

Knock, knock.

Who's there?

Tarzan.

Tarzan who?

Tarzan stripes forever.

Knock, knock.

Who's there?

Barbie.

Barbie who?

Barbie Q.

Halloween

Knock, knock.

Who's there?

Fangs.

Fangs who?

Fangs for letting me in.

Knock, knock.

Who's there?

Howl.

Howl who?

Howl you be dressing up this Halloween?

Knock, knock.

Who's there?

Witches.

Witches who?

Witches the way to go home?

Knock, knock.

Who's there?

Vampire.

Vampire who?

The Vampire State Building.

Knock, knock.

Who's there?

Thumping.

Thumping who?

Thumping green and thlimy is crawling up your leg.

Knock, knock.

Who's there?

Zombies.

Zombies who?

Zombies in a hive make honey, and zombies don't.

Knock, knock.

Who's there?

Atomic.

Atomic who?

I have atomic ache from eating all this candy.

Knock, knock.

Who's there?

Zelda.

Zelda who?

Zelda house—I think it's haunted!

Knock, knock.

Who's there?

Boo.

Boo who?

Don't be scared—it's only a joke!

Knock, knock.

Who's there?

Indonesia.

Indonesia who?

Spiders make me weak Indonesia.

Knock, knock.

Who's there?

Dancer.

Dancer who?

Dancer is simple; it wasn't a ghost—it was only the wind!

Knock, knock.

Who's there?

Scurry.

Scurry who?

Scurry monsters live in the swamp!

Thanksgiving

Knock, knock.

Who's there?

Turkey.

Turkey who?

Turkey, open door.

Knock, knock.

Who's there?

Annie.

Annie who?

Annie body seen the turkey?

Knock, knock.

Who's there?

Odette.

Odette who?

Odette's a big turkey!

Knock, knock.

Who's there?

Esther.

Esther who?

Esther any more cranberry sauce?

Knock, knock.

Who's there?

Pastor.

Pastor who?

Pastor mashed potatoes, please.

Knock, knock.

Who's there?

Gravy.

Gravy who?

Gravy Crockett.

Decem-*brr* Holidays

Knock, knock.

Who's there?

Dexter.

Dexter who?

"Dexter halls with boughs of holly."

Knock, knock.

Who's there?

Hair combs.

Hair combs who?

"Hair combs Santa Claus, right down Santa Claus lane!"

Knock, knock.

Who's there?

Honey.

Honey who?

Honey-kah is my favorite holiday.

Knock, knock.

Who's there?

Ho, ho.

Ho, ho, who?

Your Santa impression could use a little work!

Knock, knock.

Who's there?

Yule log.

Yule log who?

Yule log the door after you let me in, won't you?

Knock, knock.

Who's there?

Mayor.

Mayor who?

Mayor Kwanzaa be filled with peace and unity!

Knock, knock.

Who's there?

Santa.

Santa who?

Santa letter. Did you get it?

Knock, knock.

Who's there?

Delight.

Delight who?

Delight coming from de menorah is beautiful.

Knock, knock.

Who's there?

Athena.

Athena who?

Athena reindeer land on your roof.

Knock, knock.

Who's there?

Hannah.

Hannah who?

"Hannah partridge in a pear tree . . ."

Knock, knock.

Who's there?

Avery.

Avery who?

Avery merry Christmas to you!

Knock, knock.

Who's there?

Anna.

Anna who?

Anna happy new year.

Birthday

Knock, knock.

Who's there?

Hippo.

Hippo who?

Hippo birthday to you!

Knock, knock.

Who's there?

Bacon.

Bacon who?

I'm bacon a cake for your birthday.

Knock, knock.

Who's there?

Farmer.

Farmer who?

I hope I get a dog farmer birthday.

Knock, knock.

Who's there?

Osborne.

Osborne who?

Osborne today. It's my birthday.

Knock, knock.

Who's there?

Doughnut.

Doughnut who?

Doughnut open this until your birthday.

Knock, knock.

Who's there?

Frankfurter.

Frankfurter who?

Frankfurter lovely present.

GARDEN GIGGLES

Knock, knock.

Who's there?

Daisy.

Daisy who?

Daisy plays; nights he sleeps.

Knock, knock.

Who's there?

Rosa.

Rosa who?

Rosa corn grow in the field.

Knock, knock.

Who's there?

Petunia.

Petunia who?

There's a problem petunia and me.

Knock, knock.

Who's there?

Turnip.

Turnip who?

Turnip the volume. This is my favorite song!

Knock, knock.

Who's there?

Topic.

Topic who?

Topic a wildflower is against the law.

Knock, knock.

Who's there?

Tree.

Tree who?

Tree more days till vacation.

Knock, knock.

Who's there?

Violet.

Violet who?

Violet that go to waste?

Knock, knock.

Who's there?

Butternut.

Butternut who?

Butternut come in—the floor's wet.

Knock, knock.

Who's there?

Cotton.

Cotton who?

Cotton a trap—please get me out!

Knock, knock.

Who's there?

Pickle.

Pickle who?

Pickle little flower for your mother.

Knock, knock.

Who's there?

Garden.

Garden who?

Garden my gold from pirates.

Knock, knock.

Who's there?

Summertime.

Summertime who?

Summertime you can be a real pest.

Knock, knock.

Who's there?

Barley.

Barley who?

I can barley wait!

Knock, knock.

Who's there?

Weed.

Weed who?

Weed better go home—it's time for lunch.

Knock, knock.

Who's there?

Zany.

Zany who?

Zany body have some carrots? I'm hungry!

Knock, knock.

Who's there?

Thistle.

Thistle who?

Thistle be the last joke in this chapter.

LAST LAUGHS

Knock, knock.

Who's there?

Nose.

Nose who?

Nose any more knock-knock jokes?

Knock, knock.

Who's there?

Wood.

Wood who?

Wood you laugh at my jokes?

Knock, knock.

Who's there?

Ears.

Ears who?

Ears another knock-knock joke!

Knock, knock.

Who's there?

Spin.

Spin who?

Spin too long since we saw each other.

Knock, knock.

Who's there?

Police.

Police who?

Police stop telling knock-knock jokes.

Knock, knock.

Who's there?

Gable.

Gable who?

Gable to leap tall

buildings in a single bound!

Knock, knock.

Who's there?

Ooze.

Ooze who?

Ooze in charge here?

Knock, knock.

Who's there?

Goliath.

Goliath who?

Goliath down. You looketh tired.

Knock, knock.

Who's there?

Nana.

Nana who?

Nana your business!

Knock, knock.

Who's there?

You.

You who?

Did you call me?

Knock, knock.

Who's there?

Alda.

Alda who?

Alda kids like my knock-knock jokes.

Knock, knock.

Who's there?

Comet.

Comet who?

Comet a crime, go to jail.

Knock, knock.

Who's there?

Army.

Army who?

Army and you still friends?

Knock, knock.

Who's there?

Disguise.

Disguise who?

Disguise de limit.

Knock, knock.

Who's there?

Juicy.

Juicy who?

Juicy any monsters under my bed?

Knock, knock.

Who's there?

Dare.

Dare who?

Dare, dare. It's OK!

Knock, knock.

Who's there?

Sicily.

Sicily who?

Sicily question.

Knock, knock.

Who's there?

Darwin.

Darwin who?

I'll be Darwin you open the door.

Knock, knock.

Who's there?

Noel.

Noel who?

Noel bows on the table, please.

Knock, knock.

Who's there?

Toothy.

Toothy who?

Toothy is the day after Monday.

Knock, knock.

Who's there?

Sofa.

Sofa who?

Sofa, so good.

Knock, knock.

Who's there?

August.

August who?

August of wind almost blew me away!

Knock, knock.

Who's there?

Boil.

Boil who?

Boil you like this next joke!

Knock, knock.

Who's there?

Noise.

Noise who?

Noise to see you! How have you been?

Knock, knock.

Who's there?

Adair.

Adair who?

Adair once, but now I'm bald.

Knock, knock.

Who's there?

Clothesline.

Clothesline who?

Clothesline all over the floor end up wrinkled.

Knock, knock.

Who's there?

Button.

Button who?

Button in is not polite.

Knock, knock.

Who's there?

Dots.

Dots who?

Dots not important.

Knock, knock.

Who's there?

Habit.

Habit who?

Habit your way, I'll come back later.

Knock, knock.

Who's there?

Thor.

Thor who?

Thor-ry, wrong door.

Knock, knock.

Who's there?

Mission.

Mission who?

Mission you lots—wish you were here!

Knock, knock.

Who's there?

Fannie.

Fannie who?

Fannie body asks, I'm not home.

Knock, knock.

Who's there?

Congo.

Congo who?

Congo out—I'm grounded.

Knock, knock.

Who's there?

Hideout.

Hideout who?

Hideout even you thought it was possible.

Knock, knock.

Who's there?

Avenue.

Avenue who?

Avenue heard enough of these jokes?

Knock, knock.

Who's there?

Tanks.

Tanks who?

Tanks for all the laughs!